Meddli*n'* Women™

Women Who Through Their Course of Actions

Changed the Course of History

Series One: The Original MW

CAMILLE G. ITON

ISBN: 0692454055
ISBN: 978-0-692-45405-3

DEDICATION

This Book and Series is dedicated to every *Meddlin'* Woman of the Past, Present, and Future who has ever **"meddled" for good** and **for the good of mankind**; and, to the Men, Women, and Children who have had the fortune (or, *misfortune*) to have crossed paths of one of these remarkable, amazing Women.

This Book is further dedicated to the extraordinary, but often times misunderstood *Meddlin'* Women of *their times*, who through their deeds and actions impacted not only their lives, but the lives of their family and friends; their neighbors and communities; their cities and their countries, their nations and the world.

Generations of Women have come and gone, however, the names of these Women continue to live on, as do their stories through the telling and retelling by those of us who dare to learn from the "haps" and "mishaps" of these amazing Human Beings in general, and *Meddlin'* Women in particular.

To the Women who in their own right "*stuck their noses in*" at just the right time, "*intervened*" at precisely the right moment, "*eavesdropped*" on just the right occasion; to these Women, we salute, we acknowledge, and we celebrate their audacity to take action and thus risk altering the lives of hundreds or thousands, or even millions of people, just as a result of their; direct or *indirect*, their good or *not so good*, their intentional or *unintentional*, but to what nonetheless, amounts to "*Meddlin'.*"

A WORD FROM THE AUTHOR

What started in the living room in a Women's Small Group Study has reignited between the pages of this first in a series of Stories on Women, who through their course of actions changed the course of history. Book one is based on the first three chapters of the Book of Genesis from the Old Testament (Gen. 1:26 through 3:22).

The first part of the book highlights the *Original* "Meddlin' Woman written in narrative form, **like Genesis with a twist** can be read aloud in a group setting, or acted out as by several individuals in a **drama or play**. The rest of the book is intended for a Women's Small Group Study with common sense (or *horse* sense, depending on how you look at it) type questions along with room to record the reader's initial feedback, thoughts and *mixed* responses. The reading might make for some lively discussion. (Did I forget to mention, you should **pray before reading this book?**)

Regardless of the method of study that you choose to engage with this first *Meddlin'* Woman's Story, this book that you now have in your hands you are reading but for one reason, and one reason only; (Circle the one which applies to you); I am reading this book; by accident; by design; had to be fate; I found it on the internet, for some odd reason it came up when I did an engine search for "apple"; me, I got it in the mail - *with no return address*; somebody left it on *my* doorstep; somebody dropped it and I just happened to pick it up; it was my destiny; my friend recommended it; dumb bad luck; I got it on-line; Divine intervention.

Now that you do have it, should you yourself be "tempted," to tell someone else about the book, say for instance that "BFF" (Best Friend Forever) or that "TFFL" (That Friend For Live), beware, 'lest they accuse You of Meddlin'!

CONTENTS

Acknowledgements

ACKNOWLEDGMENTS

I would like to thank Michele Sims and the small group of women Erica Douglas, Tracy Clinton from the Word of God Christian Center (WOGCC) for allowing me to teach Old Testament Survey in what would become a Small Group Bible Study and hence create and sow the seed for what would later become "*Meddlin'* Women," the Series One.

I would additionally like to thank Pastor Donnie and Pastor Pat Moore of Word of God Christian Center (WOGCC) for helping me to grow my gifts. I would further like to thank the entire WOGCC Family for their fellowship and encouragement and would like to thank Minister James E. Fields for his gifts of Exhortation and Compassion and for always encouraging me and describing me as a "*Teacher's* Teacher," and giving me a nickname which was an encouragement to me.

I want to thank Pastor Mike Wilson of Grace Community Bible Church and I would like to thank all of my church families who through the years gave me support and encouragement and providing support through fervent prayer; Saidah Hatchett and her sister Betty, Donna Marion, & Theresa (Stephania) Moore; Betty (Mama B) and Maurice Braxton, Adele Braxton-Fields; Pastor Olatunde Madamidola and the HGPM Church Family; Gospel Artist Rev. Earl Stuckey, Musician Allen Webb; Rev. Charles Bennett, First Lady Mrs. Bennett and daughter Gospel Singer Connie Bennett; PCBC "Reflections" Speaker, James Iglehart; Sandra Iglehart; Cuzins'; Karen Johnson, Beth & John Berry, AJ Cy, Darryl Gordon, Lauren Yates, Larry Yates, Jamie Yates; Lisa Ivory, Krystena Lee & Jin; Great Aunt Minnie, Aunts' Florence, Betty, Adrienna, Lona, and Marie; Divine Faith Ministries International (DFMI) Bishop Donald E. Battle, Co-Pastor Gwen and Pastor Vonnie Battle; Minister Deborah Richmond, Minister DaRon Mosley & Minister Betty Vannoy; Michael "faithful" Kiah and Wanda Kiah; Katrina Hill-Gerald; Devona Gilliam, Marilyn Owsley, Arnetta Dean Williams; Della Tomlin; Emmanuel Egipciaco; Robert Silver, Bridgett and Anthony Ladd; my Dad, Kelvin Iton and Brother Tony Iton and my Mother/Greatest Fan/Juanita Iton who has not stopped loving or supporting me for over 80 years of which I am most grateful.

Most of all, I would like to thank God, my heavenly Father for His gift of Salvation through Faith in Jesus the Messiah and through the inspiration, leading, teaching and anointing of His Holy Spirit.

Meddling

To intervene, interfere, "butt in," dabble in, intrude, stir, gossip, pry (disturb), watch, sneak, busy body, nuisance, pest, "nosy parker," snoop, stick your nose in where it doesn't belong...

Meddlin'

Everything that is listed above in addition to being followed by the spoken, or unspoken, whispered or shouted, the insinuated, implied or inferred noun, Woman – as in Meddlin' Woman

CHAPTER ONE

IN THE BEGINNING

"She also gave some to her husband, who was with her, and he ate it"

Gen 3:6 (NIV)

"To Adam He said, "Because you listened to your wife and ate fruit from the tree about which I commanded you, 'You must not eat from it…'"

God – Gen 3:17 (NIV)

The woman said, "The serpent deceived me, and I ate."

Eve – Gen 3:13b (NIV)

"What Had Happened Was…"

So, there *I am* in the Garden of Eden. I'm not alone, I'm there with my husband – so *he won't be alone.* (Gen. 2:18) I am a "helper" like none other. I'm bone of his bone, and flesh of his flesh. (Gen. 2:23) And, for all intents and purposes, one could say, I'm *naked.* But, then, so is he. So why should I be ashamed? That's my <u>Husband</u>, that's "**My Man**!" In fact, neither one of us were ashamed. (Gen 2:25)

So, how this all came about was that at the time My Man came to live in the "Garden," God and My Man had a meeting (*before* I got there) (Gen 3:16-17), and they discussed the "rules" of living in the Garden, located down in Eden. Now some of the do's and the don'ts that they went over at that time was that My Man was *"commanded"* by God regarding his *place of residence* as follows; My Man was to "work it," "take care of it," and, he could eat from any tree in the Garden, <u>*except*</u> "for the tree of the knowledge of 'good and evil'," because the day My Man ate from *that* tree, he would die. (Gen 2:15-17) That's it, pretty much, other than naming a few animals, okay, more than a few, <u>*all*</u> of the animals, but, those were the *instructions.* (Gen 2:19-20) That was the *deal.* That was the *"agreement"* between God and my Man. Sounds pretty easy, don't you think? Oh, no - my Husband, he was not just the Gardener, he the Garden *Overseer,* he was responsible for overseeing not only the Garden of Eden, but every living creature as well, all, the fish in the sea, all the birds in the air, [any dinosaurs that happened to be wondering around], I mean you, name it, My Man was over it; every living creature, every last one was my Man's responsibility. (Gen 1:26-28) Wow! How exciting! My Man's first job is a Manager, a Director, an Administrator, and a Superintendent, with direct reports! Who cares if they were on all fours, some with fur, others crawling around and such, my Man was still over them! And yet, be that as it may, anybody could tell from the get go, that My Man wasn't going to be able to do all that ruling by himself, he was going to need some help! And, truthfully speaking, lots of it! That's where I come in. I'm the Help, Helper, to be exact. And, to be truthful, I was really in charge of HR (Human Resources) because as it turns out, I was also the one, the only Helper, who My Man was going to need to populate the World Dynasty, i.e., what would later become the Family Business, the business of ruling and subduing and taking care of the earth. That's okay, you can give me more than one job. I ***know*** how to multi-task. Co-ruler, Manager of HR (Human Resources), no problem.

So one day I'm doing my morning exercise, right, (one to two hours every morning), and I must have been walking backwards you know (that is so good for you, walking backwards, you know it's said to prevent hunchback), so as I was saying, I'm walking backwards, which is the only reason I found myself right in front of that tree that God told My Man, Adam, not to eat from. I'm just *mindin' my own business,* doing leg squats and some arm circles when the *Serpent,* also one of God's creations, who *for some unknown reason* (at least I didn't know the reason), started to strike up a conversation with me! And, so now this here, *Serpent,* who I didn't know at the time, first time we met, it seemed to me like he was kind of cunning, acting kind of sneaky and *"serpenty"* and all and here he is trying to talk to me behind my Husband's back. I know, I shouldn't have even entertained having a conversation with that 'ole *Serpent,* but I did, I listened, for it appeared he had a "theological" question that he wanted to ask me, i.e. a question about God. And, me, well, to let him know there was more to me than just beauty (wink), I mean I had brains, too, I, therefore, chose to answer the question, that is, to the best of my ability. Well, how was I to know that he was "scheming" on me? So now then the *Serpent* directed his question to me, he said to me, "Did God really say, 'You must not eat from any tree in the garden'?" (Gen 3:1) And, to be honest, just the way that he asked me that, it was like he, the *Serpent* was in awe of the situation. I mean he acted like he couldn't believe it. Not eat of every tree? Well, you know, it was like he just didn't understand, why we, my Husband and I did not have "full access" to the Garden. (And, I guess it was like if he questioned it, well then maybe I should be questioning it, too, right?) Well, so then, I began to *"break it down"* to the *Serpent* and I told him, let me tell you how it is and what it is that God said. And, so, like yeah, I proceeded to respond to the *Serpent* (I'm a tell him all of what God said, like because obviously he wasn't at the "the meeting"). I told him we may eat the fruit from the trees in the Garden, but the fruit of the tree in the middle of the Garden, that's what God said we cannot eat it, and, in fact, better not even touch it, [I may have been exaggerating, just a tad] or else, [God said] YOU WILL DIE!.(Gen 3:2-3)

So now I've answered the question! Cased closed, right? No, he, the *Serpent,* he wants to clue me in, he's gonna "school" me, and tell me **what's really going on**! You not gonna die, the *Serpent* tells me. No, in fact, what God didn't tell you (insinuating now that God is keeping something from me because He didn't want me and My Man to know) that when you <u>eat the fruit</u>, "your eyes will be opened and you will be [just] like God, and (not to mention), you will know good and evil," (which makes, sense, right?) It was the fruit <u>*from the tree*</u> of "Knowledge" of good and evil...) Once again, I surmised in my own flesh, I mean *mind,* that the *Serpent* was *insinuating* to me that *if you don't know good and evil,* then you ain't got it going on. Now, I *knew* that was a lie! We were Man and Woman living in Paradise, Me and My Man living the good life, oh, we had it goin' on alright! But, now the *Serpent's* words got me to thinking, and when I thought about it, with all that we had going on, maybe we could use <u>*a little more knowledge*</u> that the fruit of this tree, according to the *Serpent*, could provide. I mean, my Man had been on the job long enough that it was time for a promotion, am I right or what?

So, with all that insinuating (and deceiving), I could see for myself the fruit was good for food (*lust of the flesh*) (and all of that talk was making me hungry); the fruit looked good; (*lust of the eyes*) and at the very least by eating it, it was going to make me really smart (*pride of life*). Alright then, smarter than I already was by being created in the image of God and all. So with any luck, even if it turned out that I would not be as smart as God, at least I would know what He knows! Sounded good to me. (Shrugs shoulders) So, I ate. Yep! I made up my mind right then and there, that's what I was going to do, and I did it. Nope, I didn't ask my husband, what I should do, even though he was there. (Why did I need to ask him?) I was capable of making my own decisions. I had free will, didn't I? Same as he. And, my will is my own, is it not? After all, it was just a taste test? Looks good, taste good, good for you, what's the problem? The *Serpent* said that nothing *bad* would happen, like we wouldn't die for real, right? God didn't really mean "you will die" the way that He said it, (pausing) did He? Isn't that what the *Serpent* said? And, the *Serpent*, he would never lie to me, would he? For, he too, was created by God. What reason would he have to lie? Oh, it's just too much too *fathom* it all. I couldn't even really think about that right now, you know, it's too much to comprehend, yeah just too much going on... All I knew, is that the *Serpent*, he said that if I eat of the Tree of 'Knowledge of Good and Evil', that "my eyes would be opened," (wow, no I didn't know what that meant, but wow, anyhow) and *then* I would <u>be *like God*</u> (I wasn't sure I knew what that meant either, but it sounds AWESOME, don't it?) Not to mention even with all that, I would then know, you guessed it, good and evil! Yep, that's right! Not gonna die, my eyes opened, I'm a *be like* God, sounds like a *Win Win* to me! So, to let's cut to the chase, shall we, I ate it! That's right, me, Eve, soon to be the "Mother of all Living," **I ate the fruit** (did I say apple? Didn't nobody say nothin' about no *apple*!) I said fruit. Because it was fruit from the tree that God forbid us to eat from, which is why some referred to it as, you know, "forbidden fruit,"

What else went down, what else happened after I ate? Oh, yeah, that, well after I ate the fruit, I gave some to my Husband. I means as far as I could tell, it was time for My Husband, My Man to receive a promotion, was it not? And being like God would have definitely be a promotion, agreed? So, yes, I gave the fruit to Adam, and, yes, I knew it was Forbidden, the Fruit I mean; not the part about me giving it to him, that part was alright because I was His Helper, you know, Adam, he was My Man, my Husband, my Main Squeeze, who would be my Lifelong Partner in Paradise. And, he was right there with me, wasn't he? I didn't mean no harm, in giving him the apple, I mean fruit, (see there, you even got me calling it an apple), I just wanted him to be "Godlike," too, because, not only was we co-Partners in the "Eden Garden Business Venture," but we both was going to have to be Godlike, for this here thing to work! So, that's right, the *Serpent* did the marketing and I assisted in the distribution of what really amounted to prohibition of the forbidden fruit; fruit that was guaranteed to give us a high so great that, if the Serpent was correct, by the time we came down we see both Good and Evil. (Looking down at my feet now) Well, he didn't have to eat it, My Man, – I mean not if he didn't want to. Nobody was forcing him to eat that fruit I just thought maybe, he wanted to eat it, the same as me. Why should I take responsibility for what he did? (Looking down) I didn't make him eat it.

Changing course here, so, uh oh, so, here we go and well, yes, believe it or not, this is where the story goes downhill from here. Because you know what? Our eyes *were* opened, and me, (a.k.a., *"Ain't Got Good Sense,)"* and my-Man (a.k.a. *"Dummy")* oh yes, my eyes were *really* open now, we was, well, you know **naked**. OMGeeee, I couldn't believe it. There we are, living in Paradise, and now, for the first time, if I'm not mistaken, we are standing there, looking at each other, both of us, butt naked as a "jaybird." Well this was not going to do at all, because now, we were kind of self-conscious, you know, embarrassed and ashamed, so, I then like got my sowing skills together, pulled out my needle and thread, and together *Dummy* and I made some designer clothing out of some fig leaves, (we had to use that which we had on hand.) After which, once we had them on, come to find out, I can look just as good with my "leaves on," as I can with my "leaves off.'" Okay? So as the first two fashion designers, the two of us, My Man and I, not wanting to draw attention to ourselves, we, therefore, then went into hiding.

Well as you can imagine, the day just flew by, where did the time go, and as *fate* would have it, God was taking His evening stroll in the Garden and just happened to be wondering where we were? Well of course we are still in hiding because we, you know, *naked* and all, fig leaves or no fig leaves. So God calls my Husband and you know My Man had to answer when God called him, and told God, "I heard You in the Garden, and I was afraid, because I was *naked*, so I hid." OMGEEEE! I know he didn't just tell God that he was naked, suggesting that we now *knew* that we was "naked," which we wouldn't have known if we hadn't of eaten from the tree of you know what, from you know where, because you know who said we could and that nothing bad would happen (like my Man and I dying, for instance). So now *God* wants to know well, **who** told him he was *naked*? And before he could answer, God also asks my Husband and wanted to know if he (*Dummy*), if he had eaten from the tree that God *told* him not to eat from? And you know just by the way the question was raised, the *hairs* stood up on the back of my head... I knew we was in trouble.

I know what you're thinking, and nope, God didn't ask nothing about me, I'm saying, my name did not even come in the conversation up to this point. I was almost like, my name is West and I ain't in this mess! For you see this here conversation that was taking place right about now, just had to do with God and Man, just like that *"Agreement,"* was between God and Man, I mean my Husband, Adam, (I mean, *Dummy*).Well, yes, that agreement applied to me as well, I mean, I was after all, Woman, taken out of Man, but that's beside the point, the lawful *Agreement* itself that God made regarding not eating the fruit from that tree was with My Man, Adam. Well, instead of just saying yes, I ate the fruit from the tree you told me not to eat from, *Dummy,* said "the Woman," (meaning me, *Ain't Got Good Sense*), the Woman, – here we go "Blame it on the Woman cause it's her fault), the Woman You [meaning, God] gave to be with me, (oh, no, so now we blaming this on God are we?) Well, *that* woman, **I GAVE HIM SOME FRUIT.** Period. And then, as a result of "me" giving him the fruit, that's the reason, the only reason [like he ain't got a mind of his own] why, <u>he</u> ate it!

Now there, you have it! That's the story. That's the word, that's what happened according to My Husband, Adam.

Bottom line is this, if I, the Woman, hadn't stuck *my* nose in where it didn't belong, if only I had *not meddled*, then chances are, he, *Dummy,* would not have *disobeyed* the "commandment of God," and he, therefore, would not have eaten the fruit and hence, broken the agreement. Did you get all that? Yeah, because if I had some "snakeskin boots" right about then, it sure enough would have been time for me to have been putting them on; especially after listening to my husband's explanation to God as to why he ate the fruit from the tree that he wasn't supposed to. (You know I'm paraphrasing here, right?)

So, now, after hearing my husband's side of the story, God looks back at me and asks, His voice appeared (*at least to me*) to be a little louder than it usually is when He asked, Now, *Woman!* [no, He didn't say Woman, but it was *implied*],"WHAT IS THIS YOU HAVE DONE?"

And, in trying to collect my thoughts and remember exactly what is was that had gone down, I began slowly to recall the facts as I said, well,

What had happened was...

It was the *Serpent* (if the shoe fits...), and, well, he kinda like, **deceived** me; um, that's right, what I'm saying is that, well, he *lied,* to me! (I mean I know now from whence the saying comes *the devil is a lie!' (it's short for liar*), and, well, you see, God, because **I was <u>deceived</u>,** I ate it... you know, the fruit... that's right, from the tree, (looking down as I'm twiddling my fingers now) well you done already figured out from what tree it is.

Now from strictly an objective observer's point of view, some of you out there might be asking yourself about this time, that explains why you ate, the *Serpent* deceived you (but you' sitting up their thinking , you pausing for thought and scratching your head) the question remains, why did you give some to your husband to eat? And, that's the "age old" question isn't it. What on earth induced me to give some forbidden fruit to Adam? You say, you knew he wasn't supposed to eat that fruit either, right? Why not let Adam pick the fruit for himself. Why even get involved? And, as I said from the get go, I was his Helper, that giving him some fruit, well it seemed like a good idea at the time, remember, guaranteed promotion, he would be like God, you know, I just wanted the very best – for him. But, now, looking back on it, I would have to truthfully *surmise*, that giving him the fruit, without him asking for it does appear to have been a *mistake* on my part. (And just on a side note, you cannot imagine the confusion, and heartache and misunderstanding that *that mistake* has caused in our marriage and in our "husband and wife," Man and Woman relationship ever since.) But, having said that, I would still have to acknowledge, I mean confess … that yes, given the circumstances, it *doeth appear*, that I have been caught in what appears to be a clear cut case of, **Meddlin**

No doubt about it, no matter how one looks at it, no matter what the reason, it doesn't change the fact that, according to the record (the Word), I "*Ain't Got Good Sense*" gave "*Dummy*," I mean my Husband, the forbidden fruit. Yep, that '*ole Devil (you better believe* he made me do it) that devil he sold me a "bill of goods" and in turn, I sold my Man that same bill of goods. And, as a result, my Husband (*Dummy*) and I (*Ain't Got Good Sense*), i.e., we, a.k.a. Adam and Eve, we **disobeyed God**, right then and there, in our home, in our community, in our own backyard, in the Garden, if you will. And, in that one moment of truth, that oneness, that unique bond, that sense of "I got your back, you got mine" that we had had up unto that point; and time, well you might as well have thrown that right out the window, cause there, the Man/Woman "Love-fest" ended, the Honeymoon was over! Done. Kaput! No more. "It's a wrap!" It was good while it lasted, but no doubt about it, it was going to be a different relationship from here on out. I mean what chance did we have, when we come across our first problem, our first lover's spat and the first thing my husband does it blame everything bad that happened on me? Oh, I guess you could say that it was a mixed blessing that there was no such thing as a divorce, back in my day, because what God had put together, let no man put asunder oh no, it was going to be 'til death do us part for real. Therefore, we was just going to have to work it out. Yeah, we needed to stay together, how else could we be fruitful – and multiply? Not to mention that we needed to stay together because now we needed each other more than ever, now that we knew that there was a *Serpent* that existed in our midst, in our world and was out there trying to destroy us, well, the fact that we, Man and Woman had better join forces together, we need to stay united, we need to be on guard for that

Serpent and his half-truth's in trying to get Man in trouble with His Creator - God.

Well about this time, I believe God had heard enough, He had heard all that He needed to hear, because He didn't even ask the *Serpent* what his story was (it was as if He already knew what the *Serpent* would say, and that God was familiar with his ole' ugly Nature, too), so He, that is, God, just began to curse the *Serpent*. Oh, no, no, I don't mean God used foul language, no, He didn't swear or nothing like that, He just *cursed* the Serpent. Told him that he would be cursed of all the animals and that ole' "snake" would roll and slide (I *ain't* exaggerating here) around on his belly, and he was going to have to eat dust! That was the first judgment for that ole' snake. Then God said something about me and the *Serpent* would no longer be on good terms, (the *Serpent* pretending there in the Garden to be my BFF (best friend forever) but, no God said that we would be enemies, from here on out, and something about his "seed" (the *Serpent* was going to have children?) would strike my "heel;" but that my "seed" (we knew I would multiply) would strike his "head!" Sounds like a plan! Sounds like God, my Creator, my God, my Father, Daddy (!), *ain't* letting that old *Serpent* get away with trying to bring me and my Man down; (*Serpent*, the Lord rebuke you!) and not just down, but out, that evil *Serpent* tried to take us out, he tried to kill us, steal our lives, that *Serpent* tried to destroy us, *(John 10:10)* Man and "me, Woman!" And, for some reason, I couldn't help but think as he was slithering away, that he would be back to try again, back to try and destroy me and my family, the family of Man, you know with brother against brother, and then father against son.

Next, God turned His attention towards me and pronounced judgment on me, the Woman. Oh, I know, God is love, why would He punish and penalize me for something we all know wasn't my fault, right? Well, at least not all of my fault, I was deceived, remember? Well, be that as it may, with disobedience I learned that there's a price to be paid. I was just about to find out the cost. Creator God brought me into this world and He could take me out! (Oh, you thought you had thought of that one on your own, now did you? No that came from the real Mother of all living...) So back to my "judgment," as a result of doing what God told me not to do. I was going to now have to suffer pain when giving birth, ("doggoneit," did He not know how many children I was going to have if I was going be fruitful and multiply and populate the whole world?) And, that was just punishment number one! Number two punishment that God meted out, was that I was now going to have to submit to my Husband, so that he would now rule over me. NOOOO! God, say it ain't so! What did I do to deserve this? He chose it upon himself to eat the fruit. In fact, he was standing there the whole time, why didn't he speak up and say something to the *Serpent*! That was the time to prevent both of us from succumbing to temptation and disobeying God. Why should he be the leader??? (No, I didn't say that to God, but that's what I *was* thinking). Pain giving birth, Adam in the "driver's seat" (although neither one of us could drive at that time, but it's just the principle). Yes, at that moment, as I had planned, My Man had been promoted. He was now over me, and that, my friend, was not part of the plan. Because before, we were Joint Partners in this new Adventure, we called life. My Man is the new HNIC (Head Neanderthal in Charge).

Speaking of you know who, you know, God was now ready to pronounce His judgment on Man, and, boy you could hear a pin drop. So God started with, "Because you listened to your wife's voice…," uh oh, this I could see from the start that God was getting ready to hold Man accountable; anyway, and God said, "Because you listened to your wife's voice and ate from the tree about which I (God) had commanded you, Do not eat from, the ground is cursed because of you." (Oh dear, now we done dragged the earth into this here situation and gotten the whole world involved. Even the ground is cursed because of what Man did.) Painful toil, thorns and thistles, from the sweat of your brow, (sounds to me like it's going to be a lot harder work in terms of trying to put food on the table) because for dust we are, and to dust we will return!" Did God say we would be returning to dust? Oh, wait a minute, now, I don't even need to ask that question, because it's that there question, "did God say," that got us in this mess in the first place. So, yes, God said we would be returning back to dust, and if I know what that meant what God was saying in not so subtle terminology is that he, Adam, Man, meaning he and I, (pausing) we would die.

So to recapitulate, not only would it be hard work for Man in trying to put food on the table, but it sounds as though it God was saying, it would be all the days of Man's life, i.e. that hard work continue right up until the day Man dies, is that it? Does that sound about right? Is that what you heard God say? (I guess it was way too early and would be far too disrespectful to start talking to God about Man's retirement plan at this moment, right, but I was thinking it, for sure. Hey, I'm still thinking like Man's Helper, I can't help it, it's in my nature.) Well, part of me is sitting over thinking, I guess we had better get started on being fruitful and multiplying, and having those children, because we were going to need somebody to help take care of us in our senior years, should the time come when Adam and I couldn't work anymore. (It was either that or wait until the kids, or descendants to think up social security.)

Well, that's that then, isn't it. Not much more to say, is there? Vacation is over. The Holidays, as in "holy days," had not begun, so we could expect a lot of long work days over the next several hundred years. All that leisure time that Adam and I had in the beginning, oh, yes, back in the day, well that, too, had now come to an end. Therefore, we might as well, get to cracking. Thank God, God rested after six days, so at least we would have Saturday's off (if not in the beginning, at least later on down the road.)

But before we could get to work, I guess those fig leaf outfits that we made, I guess God knew they just wasn't going cut it; so to cover our nakedness, God made us some new "leather" outfits, oh, I don't know, it could have been "wool," I just know God made it out of animal skins to cover our nakedness. (Wait a minute. The animal's skin, how would you get that without killing the animal? Oh my, are you telling me that now, blood has to be shed, the blood of a bull, or a goat, or did you say lamb? Just to cover Man's nakedness, cover our sin, our shame due to our disobedience to God?)

Well as hopeless as it may have looked right at that moment, and believe me, things were looking pretty depressing that day, but My Man, My Husband and I were just going to have to pick ourselves back up and pull ourselves together because I knew, I knew right then and there that My Man, he was the only Man for me, naked or clothed, blue collar worker or sitting behind a desk, or working side by side, with him as the head of me, whether we live in or out of the Garden... Oh, that's right, we got kicked out of the Garden, too, I forgot to mention that, right after God gave us a new wardrobe, me and Man we had to move. No, not because we weren't fit to no longer tend the Garden, oh no, our work, our vocation, our job our calling, that didn't change, *the gifts are without repentance*, no, no my Husband was still gifted enough to tend the Garden, but we had to leave because that wasn't the *only tree,* that God didn't want us to eat from. You see, before, we didn't know good and evil, but now that we did, there was this here other tree, this Tree of Life (yes, I said Life) don't you know, and it was located in the Garden, too, and God didn't want us to eat from that tree, at least not in our current state and condition; you know, us being disobedient and sinful and all, because then what a mess that would be! And, because God knows, that Tree of Life, that too, would be a temptation for us, because let's face it, the cat was out of the bag, we were "God Commandment" lawbreakers now, there was no turning back as well as, no telling what we might do, so God just like ran us out of Eden, you know our home, the Garden. So how it went down, God said, "The man has now become like one of us, (one of us? Why is God talking in the "plural," who is He talking to?), and God said, he (meaning Man) must not be allowed to reach out his hand and take also from the tree of life and eat, and live forever." Forever? Did I hear God right? Did God say, forever? Well it was right here when I was mulling over in my mind the word and get clarification on that word "forever," that Man and I got kicked out, I mean God drove us out of the Garden, and we ended up going east, and

God put an Angel, yes, there were Angels back in our day, too, so God put this Angel, this here Cherub(im) to make sure we didn't come back. And, no this was not one of those harmless Cherubs with some halo and rosy cheeks, no this Angel was carrying a sword, a flaming one, one of those that goes back and forth, you know the kind I'm talking about, well you ain't probably never seen one, because if you had you would never forget it. Well that's how God was going to guard this next tree so you could be sure Man wasn't going to get nowhere near that Tree of Life; at least 'til maybe until God saw a change in us, which I myself, truly believed would someday happen. Oh, yes it can happen, people can change, and they can change for the better. What do you mean people don't change, they can't turn over a new leaf, well, "the devil is a lie!" With God's help; you, just like me, can, too, turn over a new leaf (no pun intended) that's right, I changed. Right after I started having children, I became thankful to God for helping me to be fruitful. Yeah, once I had stopped feeling sorry for all that we had lost and became thankful for what I now had, oh, yes, it was a change, a big fat turn-around, and if I can change, and you all came out of me, Woman, then, it goes without saying that you can change too! Oh, I believe it. You can change if you have to. You can change if you want to. Well, you're asking me, change how? Well, I mean, like if there is some characteristic, you know, that you might have, let's just say, that you got from me, or Man, same thing, and, let's just say that this characteristic, is well, not a very pleasant characteristic, in fact, it can be what we might described as downright ugly. Well we all know that God don't like ugly, so all I'm saying is that I believe that, with you, being one of my descendants, well that it is possible to change that characteristic, for example, like that in my case, it was greed and craving, just plain ole' lust; lusting after things that I didn't have, but wanted; but was not yet ready for; so I changed from lusting after things I didn't have to just being thankful for what I did have. That was it. It was at that moment, the moment when I made just one small turn around, one U-turn, one about face and instead of opening my mouth to get me in trouble, I used it to give God thanks for getting me out of trouble, and for helping me to have my children, because it was with the help of God that I gave birth to my child, so I had to thank Him. I had to thank God for helping me get through something that God said wouldn't be easy, but something that I had to go through all the same. So, yes, I changed when I learned to give thanks. I guess you could say, I had a new attitude. A new disposition, my new nature, although it was always there, coming out, and my "sweet" just got a lot sweeter, and I think my Husband even found me a lot more attractive. Because after that, I had our firstborn, he, my Husband just couldn't seem to get enough of me and we just kept being even more and more fruitful. (I'm talking grown up talk now, so you all just forgive me.) All I'm saying is that, just because we make one mistake, doesn't mean our life is over. In some cases, as in my case, life was not over, it was just beginning, and it was up to me, once again, to decide and to choose how I was going to live my life. Was I going to go through life, breaking more of God's rules and commandments, doing those things, I know God told me not to do, and disobeying God? No, I didn't want to do that, because I came to understand that disobedience is sin, and I found out, but too late, that the wages of sin is death, so, no, I don't want to go through that no more. I can and will - change. As, I said, it's not too late, I'm still breathing. My heart can begin to change, because I know God sees my heart, God is not looking at me out the outside, he knows what's on the outside, He created me, but God, my Creator, I know that He sees me, for who I am, and He knows me, for who He has called me to be; Woman, my Man's Helper, and Joint Ruler and Overseer of the Earth, and of the animals, and of every living thing, now I don't know about you, but that's who I was called to be, me, Eve, Woman, Mother of all living, [Mankind, that is], that's who I am! And, even though I had made one mistake, my first, even right then, when I was yet, standing there disobedient and all, God promised me that that was not the end, that would not be my story, me just eating some forbidden fruit, and giving some to my Husband, based on some half-truth from a *Serpent*, no, **my story** would be that the *Serpent*, his seed [offspring], would strike my heel, but that I, Woman, my seed [offspring] would strike the *Serpent's* head – now that was my story, that was my end, that was my finish, so don't you know even if it's not front page news, even if it's no longer in the headlines after "The Fall of Man," even if nobody ever believes it, that day, right there, with God as my Witness, God **changed** my story; and, if God can change my story, then you, my Descendants, God can change your story too. Yes, I believe that. I believe that He can, because, and I'll be the first to say it, I'm a Witness. If God can do it for me, He can do it for you! I don't mind, I'll say it again – I'm a Witness!

And, speaking of **FAITH**, even if I may never live to see it, the fact that God said that my "seed' the "seed" of the Woman would strike his (the *Serpent's*) head, I started to believe it, even then, that we, Mankind had already won the victory over that ole' *Serpent*; the Devil, and death, that the *Serpent* believed he had caused for me and Adam, would not forever have that sting, for God not would, but had already, found a way to undo that which that ole' evil *Serpent* had tried to do, and I believe that was to stop us from eating of the tree of life, that's what that ole' Devil tried to do and to cause God and Man's relationship to be permanently damaged, if not destroyed. The *Serpent* may have tried to split up and come between God and Man but Creator God stopped that ole' *Serpent*, right then and right there. God made a way, out of, what appeared to me and Adam appeared; a way out of no way. So, yes, I had good reason to be **THANKFUL**, and after my firstborn, I gave Him praise 'cause I figured I got at least five or six or maybe even seven hundred years ahead of me, so and if He had done so much for me up until that point, and for the victory in the end, why wait? I might as well **PRAISE** Him in advance. And, in thanking God and giving Him the Glory, it gave me that more reason to want to obey God and just be fruitful and multiply, with God's help of course. I wanted to live up to the name of the "Mother of all living," and I also had a new hope, that someday, this distorted image of me, this 'still" picture of me, a picture taken of one moment in time, this "slanted" picture that may not tell the whole story would someday be replaced with a 'new' picture of me and my Seed stomping on the head of that *Serpent*, with Man walking in his rightful place again, and King and Ruler of this here Earth, where there will be no more pain, and no more sorrow, and no more evil, but Man will be at peace, and all the animals, too, the lion laying down next to the lamb, yes, that's the Woman in the picture that I want people to see when they hear of me, and hear my story.

Yes, me, Eve, and My Man, Adam, we got it wrong, in the beginning. That's why you hear about the "Fall of Man." And no, it was not a joint decision, it was my will, and yes, Man's will, it was my right, and yes, his right, it was my choice, and yes, his choice, to obey or disobey God, it was our God given right that we inherited from God. In choosing to disobey and not do it God's, way, I admit it, we made the wrong choice, we blew it, we sinned, we got it wrong. And, because we chose disobedience against God, then that opened the door for our children [that is Cain, Abel and all of Mankind] to make some bad choices as well, because they were going to come from us, you see, and have our same disobedient and sinful nature, and no doubt about it, every last one of them did. Even though they all did not always succumb to our nature, there will be times, because we have a choice, that Man will choose to rise above his nature, do good and obey, and perhaps there will one day come a Man who will find grace in the eyes of the Lord, or one who might turn out to be one of those few and far between exceptions who is willing to believe God, take God at his Word, and God will count that one Man's for righteousness, and greatly reward Man for his Faith in God. Well, I know, you didn't ask me about all that, (I just can't help it, sometimes, talking about the great great great…grandkids, even though I *died* long before then, I heard about it. (Wink and a smile). Oh, just what did I hear? Well, no, I didn't get all the details, what I got was just got little bits and pieces, you all are going to have to just wait and ask the Prophets, because they know more than I do when it comes to what happened and what's going to happen next.

So, I guess that just about wraps it up. That's it, in a nutshell – that's my story, and I'm sticking to it.

Therefore, if one wanted to, one could understandably, I suppose, come to the conclusion that I am the Original *Meddlin' Woman*, at least in regards to what History refers to as the *Fall of Man*, if he fell, well, yeah, I guess it could be said that I *tripped* him. "Oh, yeah," I had a "*hand in it*" (both *figuratively* and *literally* speaking). but, although we *fell* from grace, yes, even though we *sinned*, don't you forget what God said about that *Serpent* and me, specifically, between our offspring, that the seed of the *Serpent* [i.e., offspring] would strike <u>my</u> <u>heel</u>, but that the seed of the Woman, [i.e., offspring] would strike <u>his</u> <u>head</u>. Sounds to me like the *Serpent* may have won this battle, but he *don't* win the war; and that *Serpent*, like all who would come against God, he'll get his comeuppance in the end; for in a conflict that may have started *in a tree*, it might just end *up on a cross*, and this battle between the *Serpent* and Man, is by no means is finished until God says, "it is finished." And, when God says "it is finished," you better believe that it is finished.

I know. There is no record that shows that I believed God, after the Fall. And, I know, that there is no record that I prayed to God either, but do you really think it possible to live several hundred more years, stay married to one man, bear children, and not utter up one prayer?

A PRAYER OF FORGIVENESS

Creator God, you alone are the Lord, you created the heavens, even the highest heavens, and all their starry host, the earth and all that is on it, the seas and all that is in them. You give life to everything, and the multitudes of heaven worship you.

God as I humbly come before you, I confess I have broken your commandment, I have disobeyed your Word. But, Lord God, to whom compassion and forgiveness belong; you, Lord God, who sees the broken hearted, who hears the humble cry, I call upon your mercy and grace, and, I ask forgiveness. I believe Lord God, my Creator that nothing on heaven or earth can separate me from your love.

And I thank you, Creator God, for your gift of life; for creating me in your image, in the image of God. I thank you for providing for me each day. I ask that you keep me from temptation, God, and deliver me from evil.

God, my Creator I pray that you would reveal yourself to me, reveal Your Will for my life, reveal how I may live a life that is pleasing to you and bring glory and honor to You, God.

I humbly pray this prayer in faith, to You oh God, my Creator, according to Your Will, in the name of Your Word.

Amen.

✦

Thank you for allowing me to step out of my "King James" box, be a little "down to earth," in this retelling of my story. I also want to thank you for your indulgence (i.e., tolerance) on those particular parts of this narrative of mine, that while were not based on the quotation of scripture in Genesis itself, however, the words spoken (or written) were based on "Faith in the Genesis account." In other words, you will find I may have elaborated and in some parts embellished parts of my narrative, however, only in the interest of retelling my story from a position of faith, (in the Genesis account); hope, (in God finishing my story and putting a period where sin and disobedience put a question mark"); and love (God's love for me and Adam and all of Mankind, His creation.)

Oh, on a final note, if I could ask you all a favor. Please if you would be so kind as to remove that picture on your wall (or in your head) that you all have of me, standing naked in front of that tree, you know the one I mean, with me and the *Serpent* in it, with me looking at, biting into, or handing an apple (I have no idea where that came from), anyway, handing an apple to my Man, Adam – please remove that picture; and if you would now, replace it with this new one, with me, Woman, you can still have the serpent in it (*I know* it makes for a little more sensationalism), but instead of being wrapped up high in a tree, this picture, is with the one of the *Serpent* in his revised state, down on the ground, down on his belly, even show the *Serpent* (representing his offspring) striking my heel, if you will, just imagine the picture, with me, Woman (representing my offspring) striking the *Serpent's* head. Show it just like God said, if you would because that would be a better reflection and more modern and up to date, not to mention, accurate picture of me - more accurate than, let's say the one you have now, you know, the one with me standing by the tree, with an apple in my hand, all naked and stuff. Enough said. Would you do that for me? You would? Because if you did that, and we could redo my picture, both on canvas and in your mind, then that would make the time I took in retelling my story …almost worth it.

God bless you, Children

The Mother of All Living,

Eve

CHAPTER TWO

THREE KEY OBSERVATIONS

"'You will not certainly die,'" the Serpent said to the woman..."

Gen 3:4 (NIV)

"For God knows that when you eat it your eyes will be opened, and you will be like God, knowing good and evil."

Serpent – Gen 3:5 (NIV)

Three key observations of where the "Original" Meddlin' Woman erred, stumbled, blundered, and yes, made her mistake:

OBSERVATION ONE

She took the word of a "*serpent*" over the Word of God.

OBSERVATION TWO

She made her decision, based upon some misinformation, a half-truth, or rather in laymen's terms, "*a lie.*"

The information that she received from a "<u>not</u> <u>even</u> <u>human</u>" creature whose underlined intent was always to mislead, misinform, misrepresent, and, yes, intentionally deceive the *unsuspecting* "First Lady" of Eden."

The fact that Eve took as verbatim (i.e., as fact) the information that this "*Serpent*" creature told her is an issue. It's an issue because what the *Serpent* said **contradicted** what God said. The possibility that the *Serpent* had intentionally wanted to set up and ambush Eve and her husband was a possibility that Eve may have never considered. That Eve, innocently assumed that this Creature, *whoever* he was, (that appeared to her in the form of a *Serpent*) was looking out for the best interest of "Mankind," she did not suspect the "not even human" *Serpent* to do what he did; what no human would ever do to another human (there were only the two of them there at the time), and that is, to persuade them to take an action that would all but guarantee their death, and ruin their righteous relationship with their Creator; God. This miscalculation would ultimately result in their immediate expulsion from the place they had come to call home, the Garden of Eden [a.k.a. Paradise]. We could be pretty safe in assuming that Eve wasn't expecting all that as a result from a seemingly innocent question- "Did God say?"

Woman may not have been ready to come into the knowledge of good and evil." It could be why God didn't want her and her husband eating the fruit in the first place, because they were not yet prepared to deal with all that which goes along with "knowing good and evil?"

OBSERVATION THREE

She did not wait on God, but acted impulsively in relation to disobeying God's commandment; in her decision to act independently, she perhaps may have acted too quickly, not taking in to account whether she should ask God for guidance, and/or clarification in her decision making process; for example; she might have simply asked God, what is the working definition of the Command "do not eat?" before taking a bite out of the apple, I mean fruit, taking a bite of the forbidden fruit. Did the definition of do not eat include; we can't "smell it," "feel it," can we "lick it," "chew it," then "spit it" out – I mean really, just precisely what does "not eat of it, what exactly does that cover?

As a follow up question, Eve might have asked God, "What exactly do you mean by "die"? We talking "die now" or "die later?" Dead for a short period or are we talking "dead forever?" Will this involve a "painful" death (because up to now, I don't remember experiencing any, pain); or is this death to be experienced in the natural, in the spiritual, death by "hypothesis?" can you explain "you will die" just a little more clearly, God?

And one final question, the Woman might have waited to ask God is that, "if we die, will we live again? Because God, you won't ever die, will you? And we were created in Your image, were we not? All I'm asking is - is there any room to "negotiate," is this agreement, is it written in stone, as in stone tablets, or is there any "wiggle" room, or do you foresee this agreement as having been written in blood?"

"Whaddif's"

What if Eve had just <u>stepped</u> <u>back</u> for a moment, and had not been so quick to disregard God's Word and accept as true, the word of some *Serpent* moonlighting in the Garden, purporting to know God's Word *and* the *meaning* of God's Word better than God Himself?

What if Eve had just trusted God enough to wait on Him and ask God directly regarding any questions she may have had surrounding His Commandment?

What if there was a tree that God told us not to eat from, I wonder how long it we be before we, like Eve not only ate from it, but invited our friends and family to eat from it as well. And, what if we didn't understand why we couldn't eat from that particular tree, who would we turn to for clarification, God or a talking *Serpent*?

We know that Eve did not wait on God to get any questions she may have had surrounding God's Commandment answered in a way that would have made it perfectly clear what "thou shalt not eat" meant. **How long would you be willing to wait for God to give you an answer** regarding some questions you may have surrounding His Commandments? And---

"WHAT TREE IS IN YOUR GARDEN THAT GOD TOLD YOU NOT TO EAT FROM?"

CHAPTER THREE

FORBIDDEN FRUIT

"What Tree is in Your Garden,
That God Told You Not to Eat from?"
Camille G. Iton

QUESTIONS FROM THE OUTSIDE – LOOKING IN

As someone from the outside looking in, someone from the present looking back, and as someone who just "heard about it" versus someone who was actually there (before "Kodak" and "Polaroid", tape recorders and video cameras; cell phones and "selfies"), there are a number of questions that each of us might have about Adam and Eve and the Book of Genesis account of the "Fall of Man."

Questions that have been asked countless of times, by millions of people, all of whom have either heard or read the account of the of the Fall of Man narrative from the Book of Genesis. I have included a few of my own questions. Which of the following questions would also be your questions as well? Is there one question that stands out from the rest? And, if you could ask only one question, which one would it be?

Question One

Could all of the animals talk in the Garden? Or, was it just the Serpent? Was it strange for a "serpent" to be talking at all? Did all the animals speak and just strike up a conversation with the Man or the Woman when they came walking by? Was that something unusual, out of the ordinary, or was it just commonplace, something that Man and Woman experienced on a regular basis while living in Paradise?

Think about it, those same animals that Adam named, could respond and say to Adam, "why'd you name me that for?" Couldn't you think of anything better?

A PENNY FOR YOUR THOUGHTS

_____

_____

_____

_____

_____

_____

_____

_____

_____

_____

_____

_____

Question Two

About the Tree - how did "Eve" and *her* Man, *her* Husband, Adam, end up in front of the Tree in the first place? Why is it that the Tree that neither of them was supposed to be eating from was all of a sudden within reaching distance?

Was the Tree located in a central location (the middle of the Garden) where Adam and Eve would have to pass it every day? Had they ever come across the Tree before, or was this the first time? Had the *Serpent* always been in that particular tree, and if so, what was he doing in a tree that God forbade Man not to eat out of?

What Tree is in your Garden that God told 'You" not to eat from?

A PENNY FOR YOUR THOUGHTS

_____

_____

_____

_____

_____

_____

_____

_____

_____

_____

_____

_____

Question Three

How did Adam *interpret* his new instructions from God of "you are to now "rule" over your wife, Eve? What was Man's understanding of the definition of "rule," then - and now?

A PENNY FOR YOUR THOUGHTS

_____

_____

_____

_____

_____

_____

_____

_____

_____

_____

_____

Question Four

Why do you think that although God told Adam and Eve that the day they ate of the fruit, they would die, they continued to live?

A PENNY FOR YOUR THOUGHTS

_____

_____

_____

_____

_____

_____

_____

_____

_____

_____

_____

_____

_____

Question Five

If Adam was there with Eve during the time that Eve was having the conversation with the *Serpent*, why do you think he kept quiet?

A Penny for Your Thoughts

_____

_____

_____

_____

_____

_____

_____

_____

_____

_____

_____

_____

Question Six

Why do you think the fig leaves were not sufficient to cover the Man and Woman in their nakedness? Why did it take animal skins?

A PENNY FOR YOUR THOUGHTS

_____

_____

_____

_____

_____

_____

_____

_____

_____

_____

_____

Question Seven

How big a role do you believe **faith** played in Eve's decision making process of whether to obey or disobey God in whether to eat or not eat the Forbidden Fruit? How big a role does **faith** play in **your** decision making process to obey or disobey God?

A PENNY FOR YOUR THOUGHTS

_____

_____

_____

_____

_____

_____

_____

_____

_____

_____

_____

_____

Question Eight

If you were come face to face with Eve right now, other than the obvious "Jay Leno" question, *"What Were You Thinking,"* what other questions would you have for Eve?

A PENNY FOR YOUR THOUGHTS

CHAPTER FOUR

LIFE'S FULL O' CONSEQUENCE

"Life's Full O' Consequence,
That Old' Devil Consequence"

("Cabin in the Sky") E.Y. "Yip" Harburg

Some _Unexpected_ Meddlin' Consequences
(Found in Genesis 3:14-19)

❖ THE *SERPENT* –

➤ The *Serpent* becomes the most cursed of all the animals

➤ Physical Appearance Changed – The *Serpent* will now crawl on his belly and eat dust! (Makes you wonder how did he look before?)

➤ Enmity between he and the Women; Forever <u>enemies</u>; from here on the *Serpent* will be known to the Woman as an Adversary; that includes the "*Serpent's* offspring" (seed) and the "Woman's offspring (seed)."

➤ The *seed* [offspring] of the *Serpent* would **"strike the heel"** of the *Woman*, but the *Seed* of the *Woman* would **"crush the head"** of the *Serpent*. That's an unexpected consequence that the three of them (Man, Woman and the *Serpent*) did not expect. It's quite possible that at least two of the three (Man and Woman) had no idea what that [strike the heel and crush the head] even meant. How would I know that? Because there exists today, Men and Women [of faith] who don't know what it means.

❖ THE WIFE

➤ Increased pain in childbearing; [painful labor during childbirth]

▪ Desire for husband "*Continued*" or unchanged desire for husband even with the potential pain that will now come as a result of that desire (labor pains when giving birth)

➤ Adam is now the new "HNIC" (Head Neanderthal in Charge)

❖ THE MAN – by the Sweat of your brow you will eat your food

➤ The Ground is Cursed

➤ Painful labor to produce food; Painful toil all the days of Man's life

❖ THE GARDEN

  ➢ Off limits

  ➢ No more Living in Paradise for Adam and Eve

❖ THE CHANGE IN DRESS CODE

  ➢ No more just walking around in your "birthday suit" (i.e., naked)

  ➢ Designer 'fig leaves" would not become the new "fall fashion."

  ➢ Animals would be used to cover Man's nakedness.

❖ THE CHANGE IN RELATIONSHIP BETWEEN MAN & WOMAN, HUSBAND & WIFE

  ➢ Man given the authority to now "rule" over the Woman (since She was the one who was *"Deceived"*… and to perhaps avoid any additional *"Garden"* Mishaps or *"In the Beginning"* Catastrophes)

The One _Expected_ Meddlin' Consequence

  ❖ You will die –

From the dust you came, to the dust you will return.

CHAPTER FIVE

THE MEDDLIN' "SCALE-O-METER"

See how you fare and to what degree of Meddlin' DNA that you just may have inherited when you take the *"Art of Persuasion"* Meddlin' Woman's "Scale-O-Meter."

Where, you come out on the scale, no, I don't need to know, because, that would be meddlin'…

Based on the questions below, on a Scale of 1 to 10, 10 being the highest, see where you come in and to what degree you would be found guilty of "meddllin'."

The following are questions that can be answered with; Yes, No; Good, Bad, Don't Know, and "What the Heck?" There are no Right or Wrong Answers, **only True or False Responses**.

Scale-O-Meter Questions

1. Based on *your* knowledge of God's Commandments, have you ever persuaded or convinced someone you know or care about to engage in or join you in an activity that you knew was contrary to God's Word? Contrary to God's Will? Contrary to God's Law?

    Yes   No   Don't Know   "What the Heck?"

2. What was the result of your action(s)?

    Good   Bad   Don't Know   "What the Heck?"

3. What were the consequences - for you?

    Good   Bad   Don't Know   "What the Heck?"

4. What were the consequences - for them?

    Good   Bad   Don't Know   "What the Heck?"

5. How did that affect the relationship between the two of you change from that moment on?

    Good   Bad   Don't Know   "What the Heck?"

6. Could you see a different outcome if you had not meddled in some form of persuasion?

    Yes   No   Don't Know   "What the Heck?"

7. What do you think made you want to meddle' in the first place?

GIVE IT SOME THOUGHT, AND THEN ELABORATE:

_____

_____

_____

_____

_____

_____

_____

_____

_____

_____

_____

_____

8. What could you see yourself doing differently in the future from disobeying God and breaking God's law to obeying God and remaining faithful to His Word?

GIVE IT SOME THOUGHT, AND THEN ELABORATE:

_____

_____

_____

_____

_____

_____

_____

_____

_____

_____

_____

_____

9.   What did you learn from that particular Meddlin' experience?

GIVE IT SOME THOUGHT, AND THEN ELABORATE:

_____

_____

_____

_____

_____

_____

_____

_____

_____

_____

_____

_____

10. Can you list **any** other examples of Meddlin' that you may have been involved in – from persuading someone (a friend, a family member, classmate or co-worker for example) to take action (for good or *not* so good), or persuading that friend, family member, classmate or co-worker through giving your *personal opinion* in a way that encouraged another to take action (for good or *not* so good) in their own life?

GIVE IT SOME THOUGHT, AND THEN ELABORATE:

_____

_____

_____

_____

_____

_____

_____

_____

_____

_____

Meddlin' Woman Scale-o-meter Results

If your answer to Question number one was yes, you scored a 10 on the Meddlin' Woman scale.

If your answer to Question number one was no, one of the following three is true;

1. You are lying (That is to say you are not being truthful)

2. You don't enlist others to join you when disobeying the Commandments of God.

3. And, one last possible reason you answered no to Question number one is:

    You are not a descendant of the Original Meddlin' Woman, Eve.

For those of us who you who are descendants of Eve, please see below the first Meddlin' Woman Proverb.

✦

FIRST *MEDDLIN'* WOMAN PROVERB

"Don't let the devil *use* ya!"
- *Eve, Wife* of Adam, and *Mother* of All Living

CHAPTER SIX

THE "MEDDLIN' CASE" AGAINST EVE

Is There a Case against Eve? Let's see.

The specific act of "meddlin'" that Eve has been charged with is giving Man some forbidden fruit <u>without</u> <u>him</u> <u>asking</u> <u>for</u> <u>it</u>. Notice she is not being charged with "believing the lie" that the *Serpent* told her. The as to "why" she did it, [gave the Man the fruit] does not come into play so much as the "fact" that she did it. Instead of allowing her Husband, "My-Man," Adam, to disobey the commandment of God for himself, Eve took it upon herself to "pass him" the fruit which was forbidden by God for them to eat. Eve might have thought that she was perhaps "helping," her husband, in which case she could be charged with and found guilty of (in the Court of Public Opinion) aiding and abetting the Man to disobey the Commandment he received directly from God. It was not as if Adam received the Commandment on some tablets of stone or something, or had the Commandments handed down to him through his forefathers; from generation to generation, no, Adam received God's Commandment presumably right there in the Garden and presumably in person, whether or not face to face. The fact that the record shows that Adam received the instructions *prior* to Eve getting there, and perhaps even received *separately* from Eve, does not change the fact that at some point and time, Eve did receive those instructions evidenced by the fact she was able to repeat them verbatim to the *Serpent*. To be fair, we should not really say verbatim, in that, while it hasn't been proven, Eve may have sorta' —"ad-libbed," when replying to the *Serpent*. By ad-lib, I am referring of course to Eve saying, "we may not touch it" in referring to the Tree of Knowledge of Good and Evil, otherwise they would die. God may have instructed Adam and Eve not to touch the tree, we just cannot verify her claim, in that it was not in the Historical Record [the Bible], therefore, based on conjecture, we believe Eve to either be telling the truth or exaggerating, the latter being what most historians (e.g. some theologians) believe to be the case. However, whether the two of them could touch the fruit or not, no matter because they both went beyond touch – and both ate the fruit.

Now whether or not anything happened when Eve ate the fruit, we cannot be sure, however, we can be sure that when Adam ate the fruit, the deed was done, the act of disobedience accomplished and their eyes were opened. Additionally, whether or not Adam would have ever taken the fruit from the tree and eaten the fruit on his own, without the assistance of his Wife, the narrative doesn't say, nor does it even give a hint so we may never know the true answer to that question; however, based on what we know so far, the case against Eve does seem to be pretty "air tight," - and I would think that we do have enough evidence to proceed.

At issue, Eve's ability to be deceived, because although she was told something that contradicted God's Word, Eve never questioned it, and, therefore proved to be, as the *Serpent* might have already suspected, as gullible and naïve, not to mention as *innocent* as she *apparently* looked to the *Serpent*. The fact that Eve was susceptible to the *Serpent* was **only because** she dared to believe the *Serpent,* and take what the *Serpent* said to her at face value. As far as the *Serpent* was concerned, he had lied to the "right" Partner. For now, not only had the *Devil* succeeded in convincing Eve the half-truth lie that he had told her, but that she in turn would convince the other half [of Mankind], who understandably had complete trust in her, into believing that same lie.

Now if we cross examine Eve, other than Eve blaming her predicament on that *"ole' lying Devil,"* how much at fault might we find that can be assigned and attributed to Eve herself? Notice nowhere in the narrative is it recorded that the *Serpent* suggested Eve give the forbidden fruit to her Husband; all the *Serpent,* suggested was that it would be okay to eat of the fruit because they, her and Man, would not die. Thus, what Eve failed to realize that death was not the issue, **disobedience and obeying God's commandment**, that, was the issue. At stake was Eve's **faith** in God and whether to believe the *Word* of God or the *half-truth* of a *Serpent,* that was the true test, if you will, that Eve was facing in her decision making process –believe God or not. Unfortunately, Eve chose the "or not" option; and although she had chosen to disobey God, the *Deceiver* may still not have scored a victory over Man, had Eve at that point chose not to involve her Husband in what would become her defining moment and first act of defiance. For in entangling Man to engage in his own act of defiance this changed the right course of both Man and Women from being in "right relationship" with their Creator to being on a collision course with God. From the moment **Eve went from "participation to solicitation,"** the "die had been cast," the "clock had been set," the "wheels were already in motion" for "Mankind" to set a date with death. And as death prepared itself to become the ticking clock as a result of "Mankind's disobedience to God, the page turned, and Eve becomes forever embroidered in the fabric of our lives; with her being embedded within the deep recesses of our minds as somehow being "the One" responsible for and being caught up in that unfortunate turn of events known throughout Biblical World History as the *"Fall of Man."*

The *"Fall of Man"* narrative as told in the Book of Genesis in the Old Testament is a story that has been passed down generation after generation – a story told in many different ways; by many different people; from storytellers with many different backgrounds; where a particular *emphasis of the story* may vary and be dependent upon a particular *bias* of the storyteller; e.g., as to whether Eve was fair or tanned, curly hair or straight; full lipped or thin; eyes with an epicanthic fold or round; with a nose that was aquiline ("hook nose") or platyrrhine (flat, broad nose); or the story may be told entirely different based upon one's language, one's background, one's cultural or religious beliefs – all of these which may play a part in how one *views* and *tells* the story of "Eve *and* Adam," [Adam and Eve, if you prefer, because you feel more comfortable saying his name first because that's the way you've always heard it and it sounds it's more familiar], in addition, all of the above may play a part in how all the related stories are told, e.g., the "Original Sin," and the "Fall of Man." All having different reasons for "angling" Eve's story, *slanting* it "just right," - just enough to ensure that it's a story reflecting the image of a **"seductress woman"** being **deceived** by a **"cunning snake,"** after which, the woman then using her **"feminine wiles"** on her so-called **"unsuspecting husband"** who just **"couldn't say no"** after being **"tempted"** by such a **"vision of beauty"** and who **"ultimately' is responsible"** for him **"doing something"** that he **"never should have,"** (some say **"never would have,"** done), – if it had not been on account of that – Woman – that "Helper" Woman; that "Created From the Side of Man" Woman; that "Formed from the Rib of Man" Woman; that "flesh of my flesh and bone of my bones" Woman; and, yes, having the wonderful distinction of having been that "Deceived *First*" Woman; that "Eve" Woman; you know the Woman I'm talking about, that "I gave the fruit to the Man" *Meddlin'* Woman.

✦

The end result of all of this is that now perhaps, this story, Eve's story, has now "biblically" provided an explanation to the whole of Mankind as to why men have to work so hard; why women have pain in childbirth; and why men have to beware of the "wiles" of the woman.

How the Woman Went From Being the "Tempted" to the "Tempter"

You say that the last statement "why men have to beware of the "wiles" of the woman," is not true? Hmmmm… well, let's just see shall we? (This is why nobody likes an investigation – there's no telling what will come out.)

So if the statement, the "Tempted" has now become the "Tempter," does not hold true, than we must ask the question then, why is it that the Woman needs to remain "appropriately" covered (your definition of "covered" dependent upon your culture, could range from anything from tops and bottom to bottoms only; from above the knees to below the ankle; from barely nothing to covered head to toe) – but covered, none the less, just because when she's *inappropriately* covered, or "naked," a man just might be likely to do *anything* the Woman suggests, and hence get the Man into world of trouble? Would that be the reason (other than the "Law of Moses" in Deuteronomy 22) that a Woman's dress code would be dress in such a manner so as not to Tempt a Man?

Could further investigation into this story of whether Eve "meddled" or not, could by some stretch of the imagination also come to explain as to why at some point and time in history, Women not only became "unequal" to Man, although let the Record show (the Bible) that they were created as such; but just when and "who" decided that the Woman could be treated not only "unequal," but in some places, **"less human,"** than the Man? For we see for some reason, just being born a Woman, potentially subjects you to a list of "Woman Shall Not's" depending upon which part of the world you were born. I have jotted down "just a few" of the "Woman Shall Not's" that History has recorded might have applied to you at some time or another in some part of the world **JUST** because you are, say - a Woman.

A Few "Woman Shall Not's"

What do I mean by "Woman Shall Not's?" Well these would be written, (or unwritten) laws or traditions that were (or still are) acceptable practices that existed (or still exist) at some point and time in history in one part of the world or another that have applied typically to who but the - Woman?

- The Woman shall not own property in their own name

- The Woman shall not vote

- The Woman shall not receive the same pay as the Man of who's side she was taken (i.e., she's the "rib")

- The Woman shall not drive

- The Woman shall not smoke – in public

- The Woman shall not receive access to education

- The Woman shall not receive access to health care

- The Woman shall not wear pants

- The Women shall not divorce the Man without the Husband's permission

- The Woman shall not be involved in politics

- The Woman shall not teach – the Man

- The Woman shall not serve communion

Those were just to name a few of the "Woman Shall Not's" –there are without a doubt, so many more – that can be added. Whether or not these or any particular "Woman Shall Not's" can be directly linked to that "incident" in the Garden of that "Eve" Woman would be pure conjecture.

Howbeit, if it were not factually documented, I dare say, few Human Beings would believe, much less accept the fact that such treatment of one Human Being (Woman) by another Human Being (Man) would at all be possible solely because of and only due to the fact that one Human Being is by nature born – what – A Woman? Surely not?

This case of this original Meddlin' Woman would be totally preposterous, a case that no reasonable and/or logical person would be willing to believe- a story that has many different versions (e.g., Babylonian account – *Enuma Elish; Sumerian or Akkadian* accounts*)* of how this Fall of Adam, how this event actually took place; and if it were not for some Old Testament Investigators (hermeneutics), we might not ever believe this "Eve" Woman ever really existed!

The question could be raised, if not but for the incident in the Garden, if it were not for the Woman's role and her actions contributing to the "Fall of Man," why on earth in this world would Women be treated so differently, in so some cases, so horrifically by Mankind? What other reason could there be, what other reason could Man have?

If it were not for the present treatment of multitudes of Women being forced to live under the rule of "Woman Shall Not's" in so many different parts of the world today, I just might buy into the notion that somehow this Narrative; this Creation story of Man, Woman and of the "Fall of Man" might just be that - a story, a "made up" tale, a legend, a myth, passed down from generation to generation. And, yes, perhaps even a fable in which some diabolical *wizard* cast a spell upon a majority of the human race to make them believe that out of the 7.3 billion people in the world, one half of its population, in the form of Women, are responsible for all of Man's troubles, all of the trials and tribulations that Man has come to endure, as a result of an "incident," which took place in a Garden, in front of a tree; a "fruit" tree; - an "apple" fruit tree; a "forbidden" apple fruit tree; of which Woman persuaded Man to eat from, some two thousand (or several million, depending upon where you fall in to scientific belief), years ago - and as a result of that act, that decision, that one deed, Women in all parts of the world are still subjected to the most outrageous, shocking, and to what in many cases should be condemned manner of treatment by those claiming to be so-called descendants of Man who somewhere deep down in their consciousness, believes "it" to be true and therefore, this somehow justifies the mistreatment of all Women, in general, because of one Woman in particular.

However, if those same *"Exploiters"* of Women, were to truly embrace what some hold to be true, this presumably "myth, legend, fictional - but based on true life" account of Genesis, this incredible, and to some far-fetched story of the Fall of Man, if you are to believe that account, then you would also have to believe that **it is not Man descendants** and his seed that are the Woman's enemy and responsible for the mistreatment of the Woman, but it is the *Serpent's* seed and *his* descendants that are in enmity (i.e., hatred, hostility) with the Woman. Therefore, it would suffice to say that if one is at enmity with **all** Women, the *other half* of Mankind, then you might just want to "check your seed," (i.e., *your* genealogy, *your* roots) to see just whose descendant's you truly might be!

While there may be some treatments of Women that one might chalk off to as being religious or traditional or even cultural "Woman Shall Not's," (pants, driving, clothing) there would most definitely be others that would fall under the category of "not having come from Man" but could have only come from a *Serpent* using Man, and unfortunately for Women the lists somehow, but are now most definitely combined. (e.g. laws or traditions pertaining to marriage, education, and the sexual exploitation of woman and girls, (many who could be defined as children) in far too many countries in today's world.

How and why these lists of "Woman Shall Not's" of traditional, cultural or religious beliefs and *"Serpent* added" lists would become mixed together would be anyone's guess, however, if one further investigated, one might come up with a *descendant of the Serpent* as the perpetrator. This could only mean that we now have come full circle, whereas the *Serpent* once needed to use the Woman to try and bring down, destroy and kill the

"Man," now the *Serpent* uses "Man" to try and bring down, destroy and kill the "Woman," who the irony is, is the only passage through whom Man can be born. Might it just be possible that this *Serpent* might *fear* the *Seed* [offspring] of the Woman, whom God said would "crush his head?" And, just what exactly does that mean? Should that not be one of those "inquiring minds want to know" questions that Eve should have had on her "Just Ask God" Question List? Should it not also be on that "Ask God" Question List, that if through one Man's disobedience "death" entered the world, and now all Mankind has an inherited nature of disobedience, then why not through one Man's obedience could "death" not exit the world (?) and all of Mankind could inherit a new nature - of obedience? Basically, what was done could be undone. I would think that should be on the top of Eve's "Just Ask God" Question List as well.

All in all, be it the multiple and/or contradictory accounts of what actually happened "in the Garden," passed down to the generations through oral tradition, or printed books, or famous artistic masterpieces, like that of Michelangelo in the Sistine Chapel, whatever the method of documentation that lends it support to the historicity and validity that this Original Woman of Eden, Eve, **very much existed**, and not just existed but more likely than not, did in fact do that which she is accused of doing, and that is, disobeying the Creator's Commandment and enlisting her Husband to join in the "act of disobedience," [i.e., sin] resulting in not only the consequence of sin, death, but in addition, the consequence of the current day state of affairs of this "complex, tense-filled and sometimes volatile" relationship that exists between Men and Women in the world today. History, therefore, is Woman's greatest witness, and could therefore, make the case that this Woman, Eve, is in fact guilty of that which she has charged with; and that is of being, the "Original" Meddlin' Woman, who along with her Husband, Man, lost the keys to the Kingdom – Paradise. It is here where her "chapter" begins and it is here where HERstory becomes history.

✦

Having said that, History could also take the witness stand to provide ample evidence that the Woman's "meddlin'" has not always led in every case to Man's downfall, but in fact there have been many a case where the "original" call of the Woman, as "Helper," has led to the very "salvation" of Man. Calling attention to the first Woman, Eve, is not to assess blame, so much as it is to establish credibility to the fact that Woman, by nature, are uniquely capable of **transforming** the untold story of Man through what for them is the natural process of – hmmm, "meddlin'."

Is there a case to be made that Eve did in fact meddle? I think there is a case to be made, yes.

✦

WHAT CAN WE LEARN FROM THE ORIGINAL MEDDLIN' WOMAN?

One thing of a hundred million things that can be learned from Eve's story?

A Lesson in Decision Making

Stop. Slow down. What's the hurry?

Sometimes, we need to take time to **dig deeper** before we make a decision. We need take time to ask questions. When the *Serpent* says "Did God say…" would not the first question be… why is the *Serpent* talking to me? Why did the *Serpent* ask me what God said to me and my husband? Was the *Serpent* not at the meeting? If so, why is he asking me? If not, how did he know to ask the question? Did the *Serpent* think I took notes at the meeting? Otherwise, why is he asking me for a recap of what God did and did not say? Did he want me to confirm? Or, is the *Serpent* questioning God? More to the point, is he calling God a liar? Is it just me, or does the *Serpent* appear to be *twisting* the Word of God to say what the *Serpent* wants it to say, so I will do what the *Serpent* wants me to do – which is disobey God? Giving it some thought, is it truly the *Serpent* that's talking? And, number one, why am I listening? What's in it for me? What's in it for the *Serpent*?

Ask questions like, what is the *Serpent's* motive in giving me "the skinny" on what will happen if I do something that God told me not to do? Is the *Serpent* really telling me something that is in *my* best interest? Does he purport to be "looking out for me?" What will happen, for instance if I do not do what the *Serpent* is suggesting? If I choose not to do it, what are the consequences? What if I let this opportunity, if I let this moment pass? And, what's to ensure that I never run across this situation again? Will this be the last chance that I will have to commit this particular act?

If I ask God, would He answer me?

If Eve was uncertain, and doesn't know what is the truth, and whether it's the right thing to do, would Eve have thought, "If I ask God, will He tell me the answer?" **How will I know it's God who gives me the answer** and not the *Serpent*?

There's a lot more to be learned, a lot of remaining questions still to be asked, I guess that could be one reason, one might think although it's a pretty open and shut case, the truth is the case could be appealed, meaning the case could still be open…

CHAPTER SEVEN

IT'S *NOT* ALL ABOUT EVE

Have you ever made a major life changing decision based upon some "misinformation" that you received, that had an impact on your life and/or the lives of others? (*Translation* – Have you ever taken action based on a lie?)

Who gave you that information? (Now *I'm* meddlin'…)

What was it that convinced you to believe the "misinformation" (*Translation* – Was it a *half-truth* or a complete lie?)?

Did the decision you made cause you much pain, guilt, shame or embarrassment? (*Translation* – Were there any lasting effects?)

✦

When we look closely at the events leading up to what history refers to as the "Fall of Man," and we scrutinize the life of Eve and HER story within HIStory, we always want to keep in mind the possibility which exists that deep down inside there is an "Eve" that lives within all of us; perhaps, she lies dormant in some, and alive and well in others; however, that "Eve-like" naivety that exists within our nature of wanting to know more, no matter what the cost; wanting to do what we want to do, no matter what the risk; longing to test the limits, break the rules, be our own Woman (or Man;) make our own choices, right or wrong, good or bad and take the consequences whatsoever they may be, all in the name being human, and being born into a race we call Mankind.

Eve's story reminds us that not only does good and evil exist in this world, but that whether we are prepared or not, the day will come that each of us will come into contact with not only good, but evil; be that in the form of a "*Serpent*" whose intentions towards us is not righteous and whose actions are to be considered questionable at the very least, and extremely lethal at the very most; or whether we come face to face to the evil that comes in the form of a man or a woman, whose intentions towards us are, less than honorable at the very least, and a fatal threat to our lives, our very survival at the very most.

That Eve did not recognize the evil in its present form led to her deception and steered her in an act of disobedience against God. That she could not foresee what would become the cost of breaking the Commandment of God versus the benefit of gaining the knowledge of good and evil proved to be a misjudgment that would have an earth-shattering effect until the day she died.

We all have made mistakes, we all have been guilty of misjudgments; we all have broken at least one of the Commandments of God, even if we believe the Commandments *no longer* or *never did* apply to us. However, be that it may, we are only Human, and it is in our very Nature, (*compliments of Adam and Eve*) to at times miss the mark, come up short, disappoint, flunk, fail - "*backslide*." However, when that happens we must remember that we *are* Human, we are Man and Woman, created since the very beginning, in the image of God. And, as such, we have the ability to not only fail, but to succeed; not only to flunk, but to pass (*with flying colors*); not only to disappoint, but we have the ability to pleasantly surprise, bring joy to, and don't worry –be happy; we might backslide, but then we turn and persevere; we "fall down" but we "get up" (thanks "Donnie"); because that's what Man does. That's who Women are. We can sail through the air on wings; glide over the land on wheels; skate on the waters with skis; and soar to the moon via "Shuttle." That's who we are. We have the potential to bring about incredible unbelievable good, or bring about irreparable irreversible harm. It all comes down to what we choose to do, which side we decide to take. Will it be the *Serpent's*? - who I know there are some out there who still doubt his existence (even after everything Woman and Man went through). Or will we choose to obey God, who I know there are some out there who still doubt His existence (even after everything Woman and Man *go* through).

When Women come to the full understanding and the realization that **we don't have to let the *Serpent* use us**, we have a choice, we can say no, and when we make the decision to use our "art of persuasion" for the betterment of Mankind, the advancement of society, the amelioration of civilization, the enrichment of humanity, then we **take back** our influential position, our persuasive spot, our untarnished *immaculate* image, that rightful place in history, as Woman, *Meddlin'* Woman, and then some…

✦

COMING SOON

BOOK TWO IN MEDDLIN' WOMEN
SERIES ONE

EPILOGUE

WOMEN'S GROUP NEXT STEPS

Step 1 – Read the Word of God

This story is based on Genesis Chapter 1 through 3. Read the first three chapters of the Book of Genesis from the Old Testament to further your own perspective on the story of Eve. How would you tell the story?

Reading God's Word familiarizes us with who God is and gives us insight into God's relationship with Mankind, in general, and with us, in particular. God reveals Himself through His Word, so the more we study God's Word, the more we learn about God's Will. "Good" Meddlin' can never come from just reading alone, or just knowing and even memorizing the Word of God or different scriptures; however, "Good" Meddlin' must come through a combination of **Knowing**, **Believing** and *Applying* God's Word to our lives, in everyday situations. It was not enough for Eve to **know** the Commandment of God, ("do not eat…") because number one, although she knew it, she didn't believe it, and two, she couldn't apply what she didn't believe. As a result, allowing doubt to cloud her decision making process – Eve's knowledge of the Word, did not prove stronger than her temptation to test God's Word, not through an act of belief, but on the contrary, through an act of disobedience.

Step 2 – Write A Prayer of Forgiveness

In reading Chapters 1 through 3, you will find that there is no record of the Original Meddlin' Woman ever admitting to God that she did anything wrong, nor is there any record of her asking for forgiveness. You might say, well, Adam didn't say that he was sorry, or ask for God's forgiveness either. That is true, and you would be correct in saying that the Old Testament account in the Book of Genesis does not record Adam apologizing to God or asking forgiveness, however, this story and study is to focus on Eve, not Adam, therefore, we are only concerned with Eve's actions in this situation. Whether you write it in your mind and from your heart, with the pen of genuineness, honesty and humility or you write it down on paper with the ink from those same pens of genuineness, honesty and humility you, I invite you to write your own "Eve's" Prayer of Forgiveness."

Step 3 – Pray the Prayer You Just Wrote

After you write the prayer, **pray** the prayer [that you wrote on behalf of "Eve"].

Compare the prayer of forgiveness you wrote for "Eve" disobeying God's command **with a prayer you might pray for yourself** disobeying God's command. What might the two prayers have in common?

Step 4 – Believe God Heard Your Prayer Get Up & Live Forgiven

Believe God heard your prayer of "I'm sorry," and shake off any lie that the "*Serpent*" might whisper that God didn't hear you – Believe God hears **repentant** prayers **prayed in faith** and you can now get up and move forward. **Shake off the guilt** and shame of disobedience of what happened yesterday, and **live your life today**. Eve could not live the rest of her life reminiscing about the day she disobeyed God, no, Eve had to move on from that day and look to her future ahead. If Eve were to live anywhere near as long as her Husband who lived 930 years, then she had perhaps at least six or seven hundred years to live, **how miserable it would have been if she had to spend those several hundred years looking back on past failures.** Every child that she bore (in pain) was a reminder of her past failure; she needed no reminders of the day she disappointed God, the Creator. No, what **Eve needed was to get up and keep on living!** She already had God's promise that He would deal with the one who had deceived and tricked her in to sin and disobedience, the *Serpent*, and she already knew that her offspring would prevail, so Eve, could therefore look ahead with **hope** in the future of Man, as we, her descendants, can and should do the same. **Living with Hope can help in living a powerful, invigorating, revitalizing life!** Just because you make a mistake in life, doesn't mean you can't live a meaningful and fulfilling life. **Don't give up hope!** If you are Human, you are going to make mistakes. Making mistakes comes with living life –and one does not have to be a Rocket Scientist to know that **mistakes can have consequences.** However, consequences can serve as reminders not to make the same mistake twice. If, however, we should make that same mistake or any other mistake again, and again, and even again, it is **by faith** that we believe Creator God, has <u>already</u> put into place, a plan where we can once again come before Him, say we are sorry and ask for forgiveness. Some refer to that 'Plan of Forgiveness" as The **Plan of God's "Mercy and Grace."** It is a Plan all of Humanity should become well familiar with, because in this life, in a world filled with *deception*, the offspring of a *"Serpent"* and a world filled with *temptation*, **you may find that God's Plan of "Mercy and Grace" it may be the only "Plan" that matters.** So keep the faith – **literally** in God's plan. And, live life as one with Hope in God's Plan!

Step 5 – Step Forward– Obey God

We cannot turn back the hands of time, we can only move forward. If we disobeyed God yesterday in any area of our life, we can humble ourselves before God, ask God's forgiveness and get up and obey God today. **If we ate from the tree of disobedience yesterday, that does not mean we cannot eat from the tree of obedience today.** When it comes to living our lives in a manner which is in obedience to God, we must take one step at a time, one day at time. If <u>disobeying</u> the Commandment of God is a step back, then <u>obeying</u> the Commandment of God would without a doubt be a step forward. Step forward obeying God's Commandment.

We know that God told Man in the Garden that he would have to work hard for a living. Thus we can presume that "hard work" is a part of life. Yes, there is no doubt that some have to work harder than others, however, I believe most would agree that to put food on the table, someone, somewhere and to some degree had to "work."

God worked – when He created the heavens and the earth, and Man was created in God's image, so it would be expected that Man would work as well, as Man was created to have dominion of the earth that God created. However, God took a day off – to rest. And – if you believe God's Word, God commanded Man to take a day off as well. Thus, we can obey God by taking a day off from work once a week and not work ourselves to the bone. For those who can and for those who **have a choice, you discipline yourself to work - discipline yourself to rest,** for at least one day, once a week.

If disobeying God's Commandment was the basis of "bad meddlin'," then it suffices to say that by **obeying** God's Commandments, that can stir up <u>and</u> be the ingredients for some "**<u>Good Meddlin'</u>**."

Step 6 – Time to Meddle'!

Now that you have completed Steps One through Five, it's no doubt time for some "Good Meddlin'!" Take one of the "many" things that you do, and that you do well, and teach it to one to three people who don't know how to do it! Like that favorite dish that your Son loves, teach it to your Daughter-in-Law! Or the way you make that corn pudding like no one else makes that corn pudding, teach it to that friend that **loves** that corn pudding! That favorite dance that only you know how to do, teach it to that child who refuses to dance because they don't know how. Teach that Senior how to take a "selfie" on their "smart phone," teach that teen how to drive a "stick" shift; that child who loves to comb hair how to "French Braid," that awkward dresser how to style their clothes, that "plain' girl, how to put on makeup (if she's of age); you wonderful singers, teach that choir member who sings off key how to sing on pitch,. There are not enough pages to list all of the wonderful, extraordinary, the hundreds and thousands of things that you have done throughout your lifetime, and that one thing that you are really good at, share it with someone – intentionally! Now if that's not meddlin' I don't know what is!

Step 7 – And -Should You Disobey God's Commandment Again

Repeat Steps One Through Five again!

Include Step Six only when overcome with the strong urge to, you know – meddle…

www.ingramcontent.com/pod-product-compliance
Lightning Source LLC
Chambersburg PA
CBHW070457050426
42449CB00012B/3010

* 9 7 8 0 6 9 2 4 5 4 0 5 3 *